EVALUATING TEAM PERFORMANCE

A Report of the Working Group on Evaluating Team Performance

August 31, 1993

Interagency Advisory Group Committee on Performance Management and Recognition

TO THE FEDERAL HUMAN RESOURCES COMMUNITY
AND INTERESTED MANAGERS:

Attached is a report entitled "Evaluating Team Performance." It is the product of an ad hoc working group of the Office of Personnel Management's Interagency Advisory Group (IAG).

By way of background, if one were to ask Federal human resource practitioners to name the biggest challenges they face, designing and administering an effective performance appraisal system would rank at or near the top. It seems that there is no "right" way to do it, with employees, managers, unions and personnelists themselves divided on how it should be done. There have been innumerable studies, reports, monographs, consultants' advisories and academic research on the subject. Some have professed to suggest the "answer," while others have figuratively thrown in the towel, maintaining that the best system is none at all.

While perhaps it is not accurate to call it a trend, the fact that more and more organizations are utilizing TEAMS or GROUPS of employees to accomplish work (as opposed to individual employees working essentially alone) adds yet another layer of questions to an already complex topic. One might ask if team performance can be reasonably appraised, and if so, how, particularly given the traditional value we place on individual achievement?

In September of 1992, at a meeting of the IAG Committee on Performance Management and Recognition, a number of participants indicated an interest in that question. More significantly, there was a willingness expressed to form a working group to research the issue of team performance evaluation and report back to the IAG on what we found (A copy of the announcement soliciting interested parties is attached at Appendix 1.) The working group started from the premise that performance appraisal has traditionally focused on the individual, and that this approach needed to be reexamined in light of the proliferation of team-type arrangements. We also recognized that formal performance appraisal is going to be around for a while, so it might behoove us to learn as much as we can about it rather than simply lament its shortcomings.

While at the early stages we didn't know quite what it was that we were going to do, we readily agreed on what we were NOT going to attempt; i.e. identify for the entire Federal community THE RIGHT WAY to appraise team performance. We felt that a more reasonable objective would be to research the issue, collect information about how a variety of organizations approach team appraisal, and assemble all this in a form which would be useful to personnel practitioners and managers. Our intent was to provide a body of information so that those interested in the subject could learn about some of the approaches taken and gain some insights into the pro's and con's of various team appraisal methods.

Our hope is that this information resource will better assist the personnel professional and line manager in deciding what kind of approach might work best in a particular organizational environment. Perhaps you might want to pick and choose certain aspects of the different systems we describe. In any event, we hope that the information we have collected is useful to personnelists and managers in your efforts to come up with effective team appraisal systems. While there is a lot of information here, there is also a lot that we DIDN'T do. We did not, for example, look into the future and try to predict what legislative and regulatory changes might occur and how they might affect team appraisal systems. (Most of the policies and procedures we discuss in the report are permissible under current law and regulation.) Nor did we pretend to have provided legally validated measures of team performance. We have also not defined what a TEAM is. Such issues, while important, simply couldn't be captured within the scope of what we thought we could do, given the time and resources available. Subsequently, our focus is not on the definition of a team, but how to integrate team work into performance assessment.

Appendix 2 lists the Working Group members, with their agencies and phone numbers if anyone would like to discuss the report in more detail. This report is a work of the members; it is not an OPM product. Having said that, all of us wish to thank the staff of OPM's Performance Management and Incentive Awards Division for their assistance and cooperation. We might have been able to complete the report without them, but most of the potential readers would have been well into retirement by then. Special thanks go to Effie Siegel and Karen Lebing of the OPM staff for their contributions to the project. We would also like to thank the agencies which employ the Working Group members for allowing them to participate. Finally, we want to thank the variety of other people in the personnel community, both in the public and the private sector, who have assisted with this endeavor.

All in all, we had fun with this project. It was a good opportunity for us to meet and work constructively with colleagues at other agencies. Despite lively debate on some of the issues, I can say categorically that every single Working Group member totally agrees with SOME part of the Report.

We hope it makes your job a little easier.

David Orr, Chairman
Working Group on Evaluating
Team Performance

TABLE OF CONTENTS

EXECUTIVE SUMMARY

In September of 1992, the Interagency Advisory Group (IAG) Committee on Performance Management and Recognition established a working group of Federal agency representatives to research the issue of evaluating team performance. This report and the accompanying annotated bibliography are the products of that working group.

After studying both public and private sector performance management systems, the working group observed that a variety of approaches are used in interdependent work environments to assess team performance. These approaches fall along a continuum, ranging from completely individual-focused approaches to team- and/or organization-focused approaches. (A graph and matrix which depict the four benchmark approaches or "models" are included on pages "iii" and "iv".) The report begins with an introduction to the focus continuum and includes an overview of components of assessment systems that apply to all the models. Detailed chapters follow for each model outlining the specific characteristics, the optimum organizational environment, the cost-of-implementation factors, and the advantages and disadvantages, along with some examples of each.

Model #1 represents an individual-focused approach to planning and assessment in a team setting and begins the continuum. This model is very similar to traditional types of evaluation which may currently be in place in many organizations since this model uses only individual performance measurements to determine the final rating of the employee. At this point on the continuum, even though teams have been introduced into the organization, most work is still independent, the culture of the organization is still centered around the individual, teams may only be used occasionally or are very informal, and/or the climate and structure of the organization lends itself to individual planning, assessment and recognition rather than team or group assessment and recognition.

Model #2 represents a shift along the continuum towards a more team-oriented approach but still focuses on individual performance. The Model #2 approach introduces an element into employees' appraisals addressing the individual's contribution to the team. This model--as well as Models #3 and #4--is supportive of employee involvement and high-performance initiatives as found in Total Quality Management, Total Quality Leadership, or other programs which use teamwork as a process to improve organizational performance. This model can be appropriate for organizations where the nature of the work is a combination of independent and interdependent tasks but where the culture and environment focus on individual accomplishment. This approach can also be a beginning and supportive incremental step toward the long-term strategic goal of the organization to move from an individual-focused culture to a team-focused one.

The Model #3 approach represents an attempt to link team performance to individual performance by actually factoring the team's performance into the individual's performance rating. This is done by having at least one element of the individual's appraisal involve measurement of team performance, i.e. did the team meet its goals? did the team produce a quality product? does the team work well together? This approach may be used by organizations that use teamwork to

accomplish a significant portion of the work, that have well-developed teams, or that for whatever reason want to enhance teamwork.

Model #4 represents a completely organization-focused approach to planning and assessment as was practiced in the PACER SHARE demonstration project at McClellan Air Force Base in California and as promoted by Dr. W. Edwards Deming. This model lies at the end of the focus continuum with only the organization's performance evaluated. At this point on the continuum, there are no individual appraisals done or ratings given. Organizations interested in using this model should have a highly developed systematic measurement system in place, have other mechanisms for employee feedback and development, and must have a high-performance culture. Currently, Federal agencies cannot adopt this model unless it is part of a demonstration project.

This working group **does not** espouse any one model as the "correct" model to be used by all Federal agencies. We also do not suggest that organizations must progress from one model to the next. It is stressed that the choice of a performance management system will depend on the nature of the work, the culture, the environment, and the strategic plans of the organization. Employees should be involved in the development of whatever model is selected.

In summary, there are a number of approaches to evaluating team performance that an organization should consider. Choosing which approach to use should be done by weighing all the factors involved. The choice should support the mission and strategic plans of the organization.

A TYPOLOGY OF PERFORMANCE ASSESSMENT APPROACHES IN AN INTERDEPENDENT WORK ENVIRONMENT: EVALUATING TEAM PERFORMANCE

Focus Continuum	Individual Focus>------------------------------------->Team/Organization Focus			
Model	**Model #1** **Individual Assessment in a Team Setting**	**Model #2** **Employee's Contribution to the Team**	**Model #3** **Group Performance Element**	**Model #4** **No Individual Performance Assessment**
Approach	Only individual performance is addressed. (Rating has traditionally been done by the first-line supervisor.) Does **not** include elements addressing team work, even though employee is a member of a team.	Only individual performance is addressed. However, at least one appraisal element addresses the employee's contribution to the work group.	The focus is on the work group's performance. Employee appraisals use a combination of team\org'l productivity measures and individual performance measures. At least one element addresses group performance.	Performance is determined at the group level only. No individual appraisals or ratings are done. Team\org'l performance measures are used to determine group monetary awards, e.g. Gainsharing.
Example(s)	Organizations which use only individual-focused elements in the appraisal	Components of Labor, USAF; DMEC, GAO, agencies that have teams.	ASO (PMRS), Gateway 2000, Metropolitan Life, NPRDC Proposal	US West, Pacer-Share, GM Powertrain, (Deming Approach)

INTRODUCTION

A U.S. General Accounting Office (GAO) report states that sixty-eight percent of Federal agencies are using Total Quality Management (TQM) initiatives, with thirteen percent of the employees of those agencies directly involved in TQM (GAO, 1992). Because agencies using quality initiatives also tend to use teams to accomplish the work, the GAO data indicates that in many organizations managers are recognizing and capitalizing on the interdependent nature of the work in order to accomplish tasks more efficiently and effectively. Furthermore, because of the increased use of teams in both the public and the private sectors, several authors have predicted that in three years appraisals will be team-oriented rather than focused on the individual (**Productivity**, 1992; Green, 1991; Thornburg, 1991; Benson, 1992).

In light of the increased use of teams, it is important for management to adopt a performance management approach which will: (a) best assess work performance in a team setting, (b) be an integral part of the organization's strategic plans, and (c) promote improvement of the organization's performance and effectiveness.

In September of 1992, the Interagency Advisory Group (IAG) Committee on Performance Management and Recognition established a working group of agency representatives to study the issue of evaluating team performance. After much research, the working group observed that there were a variety of approaches being used in interdependent work environments to assess team performance. The working group determined that the focus of performance planning and assessment can be represented as a continuum ranging from completely individual-focused systems to team- and/or organization-focused systems. The model of performance management that an organization selects would depend on the type of work, the way work is accomplished, the culture, and the environment of the organization, among other factors. The illustration on page "iii" is a graphic representation of the focus continuum. It shows that four benchmark models have been defined to represent the approaches currently in use in the public and private sectors. The illustration on page "iv" is a matrix listing the characteristics and examples of each of the four models.

Because there were so many components of the performance management process that could be used by all the models, the report begins with an overview that discusses the options within those components that are available to personnelists, managers, and employees in designing assessment systems for interdependent work environments. Following the overview, each model is addressed separately, including a thorough definition of the model, examples of the model in practice, research findings, cost factors, advantages and disadvantages, and the optimum organizational environment for that model. The appendices include the announcement enlisting volunteers for the working group, a list of the working group members, and a list of contacts. A bibliography of the references follows.

In addition to this report, an annotated version of the bibliography has been produced as a resource to agencies that are interested in studying this subject in more depth. Most of the articles, books and references are contained in publications which can be found in general agency or public libraries. They can also be found at the OPM library at the central office located in the Theodore Roosevelt Building, 1900 E Street, NW., 5th floor, Washington, DC 20415. (Federal non-OPM employees must make arrangements through their own agency libraries for an interagency loan of these reference materials.)

Finally, the examples used in the models and the contacts listed were kind enough to allow us to cite their programs and organizations in our report. Many have offered to discuss their programs with interested parties. Appendix 3 contains a list of agency representatives who have allowed the working group to list them as contacts for their programs.

OVERVIEW

Components of Assessment Systems. This report presents four different approaches to evaluating team performance in an interdependent work environment. These approaches fall along a continuum which ranges from individual-focused assessment to team- or organization-focused assessment. Before presenting the models, however, it is necessary to discuss important aspects of performance assessment which apply to all four models: (a) elements of an effective performance management system; (b) sources of input; (c) performance measures and measurement systems; (d) rewarding performance; and (e) legal requirements and impacts on other personnel programs.

Elements of an Effective Performance Management System

In its report entitled, "Federal Performance Management: Agencies Need Greater Flexibility in Designing Their Systems," the General Accounting Office (GAO) outlines the basic elements needed for an effective performance management system. These elements (listed below) apply to the four models described in this report.

Design. The performance management program must:

- be linked to the organization's mission, strategic plan and goals;

- support sound management decisions;

- meet the needs of the user;

- assign accountability; and

- be able to be evaluated.

Process. The performance management process must:

- involve employees;

- set expectations;

- provide continuous feedback;

- distinguish levels of performance;

- appraise performance; and

- reward good performance and address poor performance.

Results of the program should:

- improve performance;

- achieve accountability; and

- promote trust (GAO, February,1993).

Sources of Input

A Variety of Sources. An organization may find that using only supervisory and management appraisal is appropriate for its climate and environment, even in a team setting. However, when the work of the organization is interdependent and/or if the strategic plan of the organization includes promoting teamwork, management may find it appropriate to consider a variety of sources of input when determining an individual's work plan and/or performance rating, e.g., the employee's customer, subordinates and/or peers. If the environment of the organization is centered around employee involvement and teams are highly developed, management may even decide to use these inputs as the final rating determinant with the supervisor's signature used as endorsement of the process. Using multiple sources of input for developing work plans and assessing performance may be an approach which could encourage the movement of the organization towards a more team-focused environment.

Factors to Consider. Tapping into other sources of input in the evaluation process--and deciding how that information is to be used--is an option that depends on the nature of the work, the organizational objectives, the culture and the environment of the organization, among other factors.

List of Sources. The sources of input listed below may be used by all the models described in this report.

- **Self appraisal**. The employee is asked to evaluate his or her own performance. The supervisor then takes the employee's comments into consideration.

- **Peers**. Peer input or peer appraisal uses the opinions, observations and/or judgments of coworkers or team members in the rating process. With peer input, the supervisor takes team members' comments and opinions into consideration when deciding the final rating. With peer appraisal, peers assign the final rating either directly through group consensus, or indirectly through score tabulation. In Federal organizations that use peer appraisal, the supervisor's signature is used as an endorsement of the process. Whether to use peer input or peer appraisal depends on many factors such as the level of team development, the acceptance of the process by employees, the communication skills and processes of the group, and the organization's strategic plans. (For example, in the case of an organization using highly-developed self-managed work teams, peer appraisal rather than peer input may be the most appropriate approach.) One argument for involving peers in the assessment process is that peers have better information

4

about the employee being rated and they can often make better judgments than the supervisor can alone (Lawler, 1990).

- **Customers** (both internal and external). With the focus of many organizations on quality and meeting customer expectations, using customer input may be an excellent way for organizations to determine what customers think about the organization's and the employee's performance. A customer survey is one way to obtain this information. Another way is to review customer suggestions and/or complaints.

- **Supervisors**. Supervisors, including upper-level management, have traditionally rated the performance of employees.

- **Subordinates**. To evaluate a supervisor's performance, subordinate input may be a useful source of information which could contribute to a more well-rounded evaluation and could also supply helpful feedback to the supervisor. This is especially valuable when the appraisal is used primarily for developmental purposes.

- **An Established Data Base**. Information about performance, whether at the individual level or the team or organizational level, can be obtained from various established data bases. In organizations that have developed quality and/or employee involvement programs, statistical process control methods used by process action teams may contain valuable information on the productivity and quality of products and services.

Multiple Sources. 360 Degree Appraisal is a method of appraising an employee's performance in which the supervisor draws on input from a variety of sources to provide valid information about the quality of that performance (including most or all of the sources listed above.) This method alters the traditional approach to performance appraisal by shifting from the hierarchically-based single rater systems commonly used today to a multi-rater concept utilizing peers, subordinates and customers. Below is an example of a Federal organization using the 360 Degree method.

- **The Defense Management Engineering College (DMEC)**. DMEC, (formerly U.S. Army Management Engineering College (AMEC)), Rock Island, Illinois, has adopted a system called the 360 Degree Performance Management System to *provide feedback to its employees. DMEC management has made the following* statement about this type of appraisal system:

"Why 360 Degree appraisals? This approach lessens the supervisory evaluative burden and better enables them to serve as performance coaches. Employees receive information which they believe is more fair, accurate, and credible while empowering them to provide meaningful input to the decisions having the most impact on their career and work life. The organization wins because decisions about organizational leadership, merit awards, promotion, placement and termination, all of which are driven by the performance management process are more valid and defensible." (See the DMEC example listed in Model #2 for more information.)

Additional Sources of Information. As a result of the Chief Financial Officer's (CFO) Act of 1990 (and other legislation that has been proposed), program managers will be developing organizational performance measures to assess the efficiency and effectiveness of their programs. With this requirement to develop organizational performance measures, Federal agencies will have additional sources of information available to managers for assessing performance. Measurement processes established by agencies may also be beneficial to managers in supplying feedback to employees in order to promote improvement and in assessing performance. Managers must be careful, however, to select organizational performance data or measurement processes which are appropriate for the individual or team level and for which the employee(s) has the ability to affect the outcome.

Performance Measures and Measurement Systems

Assessment Measures. Performance and productivity measures are a vital component of assessment. Specialists in the field of organizational performance have written about a variety of possible measurements for use in determining performance and productivity levels. Although the references used for developing this report addressed measurements which apply at the organizational level, these measurements can work equally well at the individual or group level.

Level of Measurement. Choosing at what level to measure performance is a critical step to developing valid measures. Because interdependencies are extremely difficult to measure on an individual basis, measuring individual productivity is difficult in a team setting. It would be inaccurate in most situations to measure group productivity by simply adding up individual scores because the productivity of individuals in an interdependent work environment does not add up to the productivity of the group due to other factors such as how well the group works together, how well priorities are set, and how well the personnel are coordinated and managed. Organizational productivity measures have a higher probability of being valid measures when applied to groups, not individuals, and should only be **exclusively** used to determine individual performance **under certain circumstances** (Pritchard, 1990). According to Pritchard, the only time an organizational productivity measure could correctly be used to **exclusively** determine individual performance is:

- when the workers in a unit essentially have the same job and the same work assignments but work independently of each other (i.e. electronic repairmen in a shop); or

- when the supervisor or manager is rated on how well the unit under his/her responsibility performed.

Frequently Used Performance Measures. The results of the Financial Management Service's report entitled, "Performance Measurement: Report on a Survey of Private Sector Performance Measures," indicate that both quantitative and qualitative measures are currently being used by private organizations. The report also contains a list of the most often used performance measures, as follows:

- **Resource Inputs**. Recurring resources provided for the individual's/team's/organization's product or service activities (e.g., dollars, staff, materials, etc.).

- **Work/Activity Level**. Measures that assess intermediate steps in producing outputs (e.g., number of applications in process, usage rates, inventory levels, etc.).

- **Internal Measures of Quality of Products or Services**. Measures of quality from internal sources (e.g., quantitative scores by quality reviewers, error rates, etc.).

- **External Customer Needs**. Measures of product or service expectations and enhancements by users.

- **External Customer Satisfaction**. Measures of quality and timeliness from external sources (e.g., external customer surveys, levels of complaints, etc.).

- **Timeliness of Products/Services**. Measures of intervals required to complete a task or measures based on past trends.

- **Outputs or Final Products**. Products or services produced, distributed, or provided to service population (e.g., number of customers served, number of forms processed, quantity of goods produced, etc.).

- **Financial Measures**. Comparison of planned versus actual expenditures, costs, obligations, receipts, allocations, or losses.

- **Efficiency Measures**. Measures such as cost per unit, productivity measures, ratios of direct to indirect costs, etc. (FMS, 1993).

Combining Qualitative and Quantitative Measures. Experts advise using a combination of qualitative and quantitative measures. Author Linda Thornburg (Thornburg, 1992) quotes Steven Kerr, a performance rewards expert on the faculty of the University of Michigan's Graduate School of Business, as stating:

> "Financial measures are where the rubber hits the road. But used by themselves, they are too easy to manipulate and leave employees feeling like spectators to the (work) plan rather than (work) plan participants. Operational measures can be put in place sooner, evaluated sooner and are subject to more control by employees. You need both to effectively measure (work) plan success."

Steps to Developing a Measurement System. Many processes for establishing measurement systems have been published (Thornburg, 1991; Thornburg, 1992; Johnson, 1993; Pritchard, 1990; FMS, 1993; OMB, 1992; Nickel and O'Neal, 1990; Huge, 1990; GAO, 1990). Most of these processes were developed to apply at the organizational level; however, they may be applied equally well at the team, group, or individual level. Most of the processes cited above include some, if not all, of the following steps:

- **Specific Goals**. First identify the goals and objectives in order to determine what is to be measured.

- **Indicators**. Develop performance indicators to measure the products, services and/or outcomes that have been established in the goal-setting process.

- **Develop Trust**. Employee involvement is necessary to develop trust in the measures. Employees will be more likely to accept and be motivated by measures that they have been involved in developing. This can have a significant positive effect on labor-management relations.

- **Multiple Measures and Inputs**. All the key elements of performance must be measured in order to get a true picture of the individual's/team's/organization's effectiveness and performance. A single measure will usually not adequately describe the full range of an employee's performance. For example, it is possible to choose measures which usually show good performance while eliminating other measures that indicate poor performance. Multiple measures should be used to ensure that a substantial portion of the work is covered.

- **Flexibility**. The measurement system must be sufficiently flexible to allow for change. Otherwise, individuals or groups may be rated on elements which are no longer applicable to the situation.

- **Feedback**. Feedback to the individual/team/organization allows for improvement. Without feedback, employees and managers will not know how their efforts affect the individual's/team's/organization's performance.
- **Analyze and assess the data**. Data must be carefully analyzed to insure that the correct meaning of the results is obtained.

- **It Takes Time**. Performance improvement is a long-term process; top management patience is needed (Thornburg, 1991).

Performance Measurement in the Public Sector. Several authors have addressed the different types and aspects of productivity measures needed in the public sector as opposed to the private sector (Wholey and Hatry, 1991; Hatry and Fisk, 1992; Epstein, 1992; OMB, 1992; GAO, 1990). They observe that productivity measurements will support the accountability of the organization and will also give employees and managers the information they need to improve the performance of the individual, the team, or the organization. The authors describing these measurements were speaking of organizational measurements, but these measurements may apply equally well at the individual or team level.

- **Productivity and Outcomes**. Hatry and Fisk state that in the private sector, productivity is usually measured by the ratio of the amount of output (the services or goods produced) to the amount of input (man-hours, supplies, materials, other costs of production). They conclude that the public sector needs to use productivity measures as well but that productivity should also include measurement of service effectiveness and quality. They also stress that in many public organizations it is important to work with outcomes (i.e. the impact of the program upon the individuals or groups benefiting from the program) rather than outputs.

- **Meaningful Measures**. Hatry and Fisk state that input/output ratios will become considerably more meaningful and useful to managers if the output measures represent important service products and not merely physical measures of activity. Measures must also cover a substantial portion of the work.

Difficulty in Measuring Public Sector Productivity. Wholey and Hatry agree that performance and productivity monitoring are extremely important, yet they admit that regular performance measures are difficult to establish for some programs, such as research programs. They state that other approaches such as periodic in-depth program reviews are needed for these programs instead. Wise and Agranoff (1991) state that traditional measures of research have focused primarily on quality of research products. In times of fiscal austerity, however, there is an increasing need to include measures of research efficiency and effectiveness along with quality measures. Organizational culture and characteristics play a significant role in determining what types of efficiency and effectiveness measures are most appropriate and will be most readily accepted by research scientists and managers.

Rewarding Performance

Strategic Use of Rewards. Rewarding employees for good performance is more often than not linked to the employee performance appraisal rating. Rewards can range from individual rewards and bonuses to small group or team rewards, to organizational bonus programs, such as gainsharing. All these various types of rewards can apply to each model and may be used alone or in combination. However, the strategic use of rewards and how they can reinforce desired behavior in order to achieve the goals and objectives of the organization are important factors that should be considered when selecting a performance management approach.

Individual Monetary Rewards. Most organizations recognize and reward outstanding performance by individuals. However, when interdependent work and teams are introduced into the workplace, rewarding individuals without recognizing group achievements may have negative effects on the overall performance of the organization. According to W. Edwards Deming and proponents of his philosophy, rewarding individual performance is demoralizing and has negative impacts on the performance of the organization (Deming, 1982; Scholtes, 1987). Nevertheless, there may be organizations that have an individual-focused culture and environment--and where work is independent in nature even though employees may sometimes work in teams--for which recognizing individual achievement is appropriate and supportive of the organization's goals and strategic plans (Lawler, 1990).

Group Monetary Rewards. An alternative to rewarding individual performance is to reward groups for good performance, or use group rewards in most instances, reserving individual rewards only for cases of truly outstanding individual performance and possibly done as part of a group consensus process or by group nomination. In an interdependent work environment, group rewards may be used not only to encourage employees to contribute to improved team performance but also used as part of management's strategy to encourage the organization to move towards a more team-focused environment (Lawler, 1990; Schuster and Zingheim, 1992).

- **Gainsharing**. Gainsharing is a group reward approach that shares productivity gains above a predetermined base between the organization and its employees. To be successful, management must strive for a high degree of employee commitment and participation and create a positive climate for excellence. Employees must also be able to become more involved in solving problems in productivity, quality, and service (Doyle, 1983). Gainsharing could be used by organizations which focus on the welfare and performance of the organization, not just one division, product, or operation. Equal amounts of the gains are usually shared among all employees based on predetermined and mutually satisfactory formulas. Gains in savings, productivity, reduced costs, or fewer labor hours can be used as factors in the formula for determining bonuses. Gainsharing programs can be used in the Federal government, and payments are authorized under the Incentive Awards authority (5 U.S.C. Chapter 45).

- **Developing Group Rewards Systems**. Research shows that group performance-award plans have better results when employees are involved in the design and

10

implementation of the plan, when the organization communicates about the status of the plan with employees, when the plan is consistent and fair, when rewards are timely, and when the objectives of the plan are tied to the organization's objectives (Berson-Besthoff, 1992; Masternak, 1992; Imberman, 1992; McAdams and Hawk, 1993; Thornburg, 1992; Lawler, 1990; Schuster and Zingheim, 1992).

Time Off and Nonmonetary Awards. Time-off awards and a variety of nonmonetary awards for individuals and teams are available. FPM Letters 451-10, Time-off as an Incentive Award, and FPM Letter 451-11, Nonmonetary and Monetary Incentive Awards, apply to teams as well as individuals. The awards described in these Letters are an excellent way of recognizing good performance.

Summarizing Reward Systems. In summary, if the success and mission of an organization depends primarily on the independent achievements of its employees, the organization should use an individual reward system to encourage outstanding individual performance. However, if the mission and objectives of the organization depend primarily on the performance of its teams because of the interdependence of the work, group rewards would be more appropriate. Many organizations have found that a combination of both approaches--used appropriately--has been successful.

Legal Requirements and Impacts on Other Personnel Programs

Meets Current Requirements. Models #1, #2 and most examples of #3 meet current legal requirements (5 U.S.C. Chapter 43) that **each** employee's performance be appraised against standards and that the results of performance appraisals be used as a basis for training, rewarding, reassigning, promoting, reducing in grade, retaining, and removing employees.

Does Not Meet Current Requirements. Assessment approaches which use team ratings ONLY with no individual elements included in the appraisal, as is possible in Model #3, or approaches which have abolished individual appraisal, as in Model #4, do not meet current legal requirements regarding performance appraisal
(5 U.S.C. Chapter 43). Such approaches could only be adopted in the Federal sector as part of a demonstration project. These approaches would also affect other personnel programs, including:

- **Reduction In Force (RIF)**. Under current OPM regulations (5 CFR 351), RIF retention standing is linked to the employee's length of service and individual performance rating. Using a team or organizational rating in lieu of an individual rating would give all employees on the team or in an organization the same performance rating credit in determining RIF retention.

- **Poor Performance**. Under current law (5 U.S.C. Chapter 43), an agency may reduce in grade or remove an employee for unacceptable performance. Without an individual evaluation of performance, agencies could not take action to demote or remove an employee under provisions of the law. (However, the potential for using team dynamics and peer influence to improve performance should not be overlooked.)

- **Promotion.** Under current regulations (5 CFR 335), employees rated Fully Successful or higher are eligible for career ladder promotion once they have met the time-in-grade requirements. Without an individual appraisal, promotion decisions would have to be based on other evidence of performance.

- **Individual development**. Performance appraisals are currently used as a basis for determining employee training needs. Without an individual appraisal, individual development would have to be addressed in an independent process.

The Models

Many of the components of an assessment system as listed above can vary according to the situation of an organization and the level of development of its teams. As the four models are described in the following chapters, brief mention may be made of these components, possibly recommending one source of input or type of reward over another for a particular model. However, readers are reminded that each organization should tailor its performance management approach specifically to its own needs and choose components which will best promote the strategic plans of the organization.

MODEL #1
Individual Appraisal in a Team Setting

Introduction

Definition. Model #1 represents the traditional approach to performance planning and assessment as it would be used in a team setting, where the traditional approach has usually focused on individual performance <u>only</u>.

Place on the Continuum. Model #1 lies at the beginning of the focus continuum ranging from individual-focused systems to team- or organization-focused systems because it uses <u>only</u> individual-focused elements and standards with individual-focused performance measurements to determine an employee's performance rating. Model #1 differs from Models #2, 3 and 4 in that it represents the concept of focusing all aspects of the performance assessment process on the individual, without addressing team accomplishment or team participation.

Objective. The objective of using a Model #1 approach is to measure individual performance and/or to link the results of individual performance to personnel decisions affecting individuals.

Description

<u>Characteristics</u>

A Traditional Approach Used In a Team Setting. Model #1 is a traditional, individual-focused approach to employee performance planning and assessment in a team setting. Critical elements and the measures used to determine a rating of performance are focused at the individual level. A reward program that focuses primarily on individual performance is appropriate for use with this model. However, in some organizations where employee assessment ratings are not linked to rewards, a Model #1 approach is being used successfully with a gainsharing program.

Adaptations. Since most readers will be familiar with the characteristics of a successful traditional performance management system, they are not included in this report. Instead, the emphasis will center on discussions of how current systems could be adapted to a team setting while still focusing strictly on the individual and without including a team contribution or team performance element to the appraisal. Possible process changes to a traditional performance planning and assessment system are as follows:

- **Performance Plans**. A performance plan is written for each employee. If teams have been introduced, this process could be changed from the traditional method in which the supervisor and the employee develop the plan, to have a group of

13

employees who either occupy similar positions or are members of a team prepare the performance plan, with the supervisor's approval. Customer input (i.e., what's important to the customer) may also be a valuable source of information to consider when developing a performance plan.

- **A Variety of Inputs**. A traditional individual-focused appraisal that introduces a variety of sources of input is one way of retaining the focus on individual performance but also of introducing team components into the assessment process. For example, an employee's appraisal may include only individual performance elements (with no element addressing the employee's contribution to the team) but use peer input or 360 degree appraisal. By using peer input or 360 degree appraisal, team members become involved in the planning and assessment process, and the importance of teams to the organization may be introduced and/or reinforced.

Analysis

Research Findings

Individual Appraisals Strengthen Individual Performance. The Performance Management And Recognition System Review Committee (PMRSRC) (November 1991) concluded in their report that a regular and documented individual appraisal is an integral component of assessing and strengthening individual performance. The PMRSRC reached this conclusion despite a presentation by Dr. W. Edwards Deming contending that it was not possible to rate individual performance.

Employees Prefer Individual Performance Ratings. The Survey of Federal Employees (SOFE) report issued by OPM shows that sixty-nine percent of employees prefer that their performance rating be based on individual performance, not team performance. Eighty-nine percent of employees also responded that input from the first-level supervisor should be involved to a great extent in developing performance ratings, while only eighteen percent of employees felt that co-worker input should be used to a great extent (OPM, 1992). This information indicates that employees would prefer to maintain the traditional approach of assessment; a Model #1 approach using only supervisor input seems to be the preferred choice of Federal employees. This information also indicates that if managers want to be successful in focusing performance management more on the team rather than the individual, employees must first be convinced of the advantages of a team-oriented approach; be trained in peer, customer, and/or subordinate appraisal processes; and then be involved at the earliest stages in developing changes to the traditional system.

Advantages of Using Model #1 (Individual Appraisal in a Team Setting)

14

Individual Productivity. Encourages individual achievement and productivity by recognizing and rewarding individual performance.

Minimal Changes May Be Needed. Model #1 represents either the current appraisal system (placed in a team setting) or potentially it could be a refined and enhanced version of an existing system. In the first instance, a system based on Model #1 would require minimal change from current performance management systems. Consequently, it is likely that:

- Developing a system based on Model #1 would be easier and faster than developing a totally new system.

- Implementation could be faster.

- Minimal retraining of managers, supervisors, and staff would be required; training could build on previous training and experience.

- Familiarity of many aspects of the revised system would result in a positive "comfort level", and would minimize the amount of resistance to change.

- Minimal disruption would result from instituting changes.

- The above-listed factors would result in minimal administrative cost to implement.

Tested in Court. Legal defensibility of the individual appraisal of individual performance has already been tested for more than 12 years.

Bargaining Issues. There are existing negotiated agreements, "past practices" and case law established for traditional types of appraisal systems. Bargaining patterns for Model #1-type systems are now fairly well established.

Disadvantages of Using Model #1

Lack of Employee Confidence. If employee confidence in the process is low, the use of a Model #1 approach will not likely be successful.

Competition. This approach may cause competition among individuals in order to achieve high performance ratings and may be a detriment to teamwork and team performance.

Inappropriate in Some Cases. Individual performance appraisal may not be the most appropriate option for some agencies or types of positions.

Difficult to Assess Individual Work in a Team Setting. Some employees work in an interdependent environment, and it may be difficult or impossible to accurately assess an employee's individual performance. This may result in artificial or meaningless distinctions, and/or in excessive documentation to make a compelling case for these distinctions.

May Not Be Sufficient. This model may not be able to address some of the problems identified in the current appraisal system when teams are used extensively or when management wants to recognize and reward team performance over individual performance.

Optimum Organizational Environment

Independent Work. This model works well in an organized, focused environment where employees generally work independently even though they are on a team or perform the same work activities, work toward the same objective(s), or have the same or similar position descriptions, critical elements, or performance standards.

Identifiable Goals. Deadlines, production goals, tangible work products, or other individually identifiable results/outputs are a routine part of the employee's assigned responsibilities.

Employee's Role On the Team. The employee's relationship to the team and the objectives of the team may or may not be an integral part of the employee's position of record. The employee's affiliation with the team:

- May be permanent or temporary.

- May be established formally or informally.

- May be multipurpose or single purpose.

Cost Factors

Minimal Cost. As noted previously in the discussion above, because Model #1 can be a refined and enhanced version of an existing performance appraisal system, direct and indirect costs, including loss of work hours to design and implementation activities, would be expected to be at a minimal level. If significant changes are made to the performance management system, i.e., 360 degree appraisal is introduced, costs for system design and for the delivery of training to managers, supervisors and employees would be incurred.

Summary/Comments

Summary. Model #1 represents an individual-focused approach to assessment in a team setting and begins the continuum. This model is very similar to traditional types of evaluation which may currently be in place in many organizations since this model uses only individual performance measurements to determine the final rating of the employee. At this point on the continuum, even though teams have been introduced into the organization, most work is still independent, the culture of the organization is still centered around the individual, teams may only be used occasionally or very informally, and/or the climate and structure of the organization lends itself to individual planning, assessment and recognition rather than team or group assessment and recognition.

Comments. Model #1 can represent a conservative approach to evaluation by maintaining the status quo of the established appraisal system, despite the introduction of teams into the work environment. This model may fit the goals, environment and culture of many organizations that wish to encourage and support individual achievement. This may not be the best approach, however, for organizations that have extensively incorporated teamwork into their environment and that need to encourage successful teamwork in order to improve the effectiveness and productivity of the organization.

MODEL #2
Employee's Contribution to the Team

Introduction

Definition. Model #2 represents a variation of the traditional employee assessment approach in that at least one element of an employee's work plan and appraisal addresses the employee's contribution to the team.

Place on the Continuum. Model #2 lies between Models #1 and #3 on the focus continuum which ranges from individual-focused assessment approaches, to group-focused approaches. The principal difference between Models #1 and #2 is that Model #1 focuses on the evaluation of individual performance only, with no team elements addressed, while Model #2 focuses on the evaluation of an individual's performance of independent work and includes at least one element addressing the individual's contribution to the work group or to internal group processes.

Objective. The objective of using a Model #2 approach is to recognize the individual's contribution to the team. It represents a movement along the continuum towards a more team-focused approach, but it still remains an individual-focused system. Organizations that have established teams as part of their strategic plan towards more effective organizational performance may conclude that teamwork should be addressed and promoted by their appraisal and recognition systems. These organizations may find that adding a critical element to an employee's performance plan addressing the employee's contribution to the team or to his or her improvement of teamwork skills is:

- either an adequate approach to evaluation in that it fulfills the organization's needs and matches the type of work, the culture and the environment of the organization; or

- is a supportive step towards moving the organization incrementally along the focus continuum from an individual-focused approach towards a team-focused approach.

Description

Characteristics

Team Contribution. The Model #2 approach to evaluating team performance is still individual-focused except that at least one
critical element in the individual's performance appraisal addresses the individual's contribution to the work group, to group processes, or to the improvement of group process skills. A variety of types of rewards and sources of input may be used.

Environment. The work environment is such that work is performed in teams or that group projects are performed at least some of the time.

Types of Measures. Measures of group contribution may include:

- Involvement in group-directed work activity.

- Assisting the group in the accomplishment of its objectives.

- Contributions to improved communications.

- Fostering or maintaining positive working relationships.

- Support of teamwork or team building.

- Improvement of group process skills.

Examples

U.S. Air Force. As part of their quality initiatives, the Aeronautical Systems Division of the U.S. Air Force developed team contribution elements and standards as a result of a Corrective Action Team (CAT). These elements and standards have been distributed to managers and supervisors with instruction to revise employee appraisals as necessary to ensure that subordinates' work plans are aligned with the organization's focus on productivity. The element and standard for all employees which was developed by the CAT that specifically addresses team contribution are as follows:

- "Teamwork and Customer/Supplier Relationships. Actively participates in team or group efforts to provide needed products and services as required to meet customer needs. Actively promotes the needs and requirements of the customer.
  "Standard A. Strives for maximum organizational results by co-operating with others to make team decisions work. Strengthens team effectiveness by accepting and working with others' positions, constraints and reservations. Builds constructively on the ideas and comments of others to assist the team in solving problems. Manages conflict effectively and actively supports team decisions even when other options were personally favored during discussion. Responds to factual rather than emotional arguments when resolving conflict." (USAF, 1990)

Department of Labor. More than three years ago, the Wage and Hour Division, Employment Standards Administration of the Department of Labor initiated a TQM program which includes the establishment of teams to review work activities and identify process improvements. Every National Office employee has a critical quality management performance element included in his/her appraisal. Wage and Hour field employees operate under performance standards which reflect built-in quality principles. For General Schedule (GS) employees, the standards address participation in team activities, serving on project teams, and implementing a customer service

20

focus. Performance measurement (currently done by supervisory review) focuses on the employee's participation on teams and how the employee fosters process improvements.

Department of Defense. The Defense Management Engineering College (DMEC), Rock Island, Illinois, was mentioned in the overview for its use of 360 Degree appraisal. In DMEC's appraisal process, one of the elements used to assess performance addresses the employee's contribution to the team. Ratings for a variety of predetermined elements are based on a 1-10 scale, and the tabulated rating of peers, subordinates, and customers serves as the basis of the employee's annual performance rating. The rating form includes the following element and performance indicators which specifically address team contribution:

- "Interpersonal/Team Building:
    1. Makes me feel comfortable when we communicate with each other.
    2. Is trustworthy.
    3. Is effective in group meetings.
    4. Open and approachable about problems.
    5. Contributes to a work environment wheregroup members share
        responsibility for the success or failure of the group.
    6. Supports team members' ideas.
    7. Encourages positive team spirit.
    8. Acts cooperatively.
    9. Encourages and accepts constructive criticism." (DOD Rating Form)

GAO. U.S. General Accounting Office's Performance Appraisal System for Band I and II Employees (equivalent to General Schedule grades 7 through 14) uses a critical performance dimension (with standards) entitled "Working Relationships, Teamwork, and Equal Opportunity." The element addressing teamwork and the Fully Successful standard follow.

- **Element**. "Promoting teamwork with other GAO staff, including people at all levels and in all components of GAO."

- **Fully Successful Standard**. "Demonstrates respect and concern for others to strengthen and maintain effective working relationships. Develops constructive working relationships with people whose goals, culture, background, or values differ from own. Collaborates with coworkers; adjusts to different working styles, approaches, and perspectives; expresses own views as appropriate. Accepts additional or undesirable work assignments and helps coworkers; carries a fair share of the workload. Works harmoniously with coworkers."

OPM. U.S. Office of Personnel Management, San Francisco Regional Office has compiled a list of "Sample Standards for Use in a Total Quality Management Environment." Below is one example of a standard element incorporating team contribution measures which could be used in an employee's performance appraisal:

- "Execution of Team Duties: In performing the team's work, the employee cooperates with other team members in the accomplishment of the team's

21

tasks, uses a TQM approach in improving the team's work process(es), uses customer feedback and technical knowledge to complete tasks and diagnoses problems in work processes. The employee makes recommendations for process improvement to improve customer satisfaction with the quality of the organization's product or service. The service or work product is of good quality, timely and responsive to the organization's priorities, and the team leader's and customer's requirements."

Below is an example of a standard element which could be used in a manager's or supervisor's performance appraisal:

- "Manages the Human Resources of the Organization. Willingly cooperates with team members in the accomplishment of team tasks. Effectively coordinates work and keeps team leader and team members informed of work-related and team-related issues, developments, and status. Willingly accepts opportunities to develop professional and/or technical skills in himself/herself or among his/her staff in accordance with organizational goals and customer requirements. Actively works to enhance his/her ability to contribute to process improvement activities and work team functioning." (OPM, 1992)

Analysis

Research Findings

Need to Balance Individual/Team Rewards and Recognition. The Wyatt Co., a leading compensation consulting firm, has surveyed many major corporations such as AT&T, Corning, Eastman Kodak, Federal Express, Florida Power and Light (a Deming Prize winner), Ford Motor Co., General Motors, GTE, IBM, Motorola, 3M, and Xerox, among others, regarding changes to performance management and pay systems in connection with implementing employee involvement and high-performance initiatives. One of the issues that surfaced was an interest in rewarding and recognizing individual performance and team performance. According to Wyatt, many organizations are struggling to achieve the right balance.

Organizational Characteristics. Recent literature indicates that organizations with a need to change the focus of appraisal from the individual's performance alone to include recognition of the individual's contribution to the group often have one or more of the following characteristics: (1) they accomplish some of their work using groups or teams and group work is productive; (2) they are implementing employee involvement and high-performance initiatives and want to focus performance planning, assessment and recognition efforts to some extent on groups or teams; (3) they have experienced difficulty with traditional appraisal processes and are looking for ways to invigorate the process.

Improve Productivity. Research indicates that when organizations recognize the power of teams, seek improvements in communications between work groups or organizations, or change to a focus on customer service, then productivity, efficiency, and competitiveness are enhanced. Employees tend to become more involved in on-the-job problem solving with peers and work together to develop, implement, and evaluate improvements to work processes. The modification of the appraisal system, when necessary, often follows later after employee involvement and high-performance initiatives are applied to efforts to improve work processes and product quality.

Advantages of Using Model #2 (Employee's Contribution to the Team)

Meets Requirements. This model meets all regulatory and statutory requirements.

Team Contribution is Promoted. Individuals are encouraged not only to improve their own personal work performance, but they are also encouraged to improve teamwork skills and processes which will upgrade team performance.

A Movement Towards Team Focus. If the strategy of management is to move the organization from an individual-focus to a team- or organization-focus, Model #2 represents an approach that encourages that process.

Supports Quality. This model may be compatible with organizations that have adopted quality initiatives.

Disadvantages of Using Model #2

Training Costs. Investment in training supervisors on writing elements and standards addressing team contribution will be needed.

Measurement Difficulty. There may be difficulties and a lack of experience in developing measures of an individual's contribution to the team and in designing effective processes for data collection.

Optimum Organizational Environment

Organizations may consider using a Model #2 approach to assess performance if the following conditions are in place:

- **Interdependent Work**. The organization's employees spend a significant portion of their time doing work in a team setting and the work involves a combination of independent and interdependent tasks.

- **Strategic Plans**. The strategic plans of the organization include promoting teamwork.

- **Move Along the Continuum**. Management wishes to move the organization from an individual-focused approach to a team-focused approach and wishes to do so incrementally.

Cost Factors

Minimal Cost. Some administrative time and funds may be spent training supervisors and employees on how to develop elements and measures which address the employee's contribution to the team. These costs may be minimal to moderate.

Summary/Comments

Summary. Model #2 represents a shift along the continuum towards a more team-oriented approach but still focuses on individual performance. The Model #2 approach introduces an element into employees' appraisals addressing the individual's contribution to the team. This model, as well as Models #3 and #4, is supportive of employee involvement and high-performance initiatives found in Total Quality Management, Total Quality Leadership, or other programs which use teamwork as a process to improve performance.

Comments. Model #2 can be appropriate for organizations where the nature of the work is a combination of independent and interdependent tasks but where the culture and environment focuses on individual accomplishment. This approach can also be a beginning and supportive incremental step as part of the long-term strategic plan of the organization to move from an individual-focused culture to a team-focused one.

MODEL #3
Group Performance Element

Introduction

Definition. Model #3 is an approach to performance planning and assessment which includes at least one element in the employee's work plan and appraisal that addresses team performance. Consequently, the performance of the team is factored into the rating system, affecting the employee's final rating of record.

Place on the Continuum. Model #3 lies between Models #2 and #4 on a focus continuum that ranges from individual-focused assessment to group-focused assessment. The principal difference between Model #2 and Model #3 is that the focus of Model #2 is still on the individual while the focus of Model #3 has moved to the team. In a Model #3 approach, at least one critical element (possibly all) of an individual's performance appraisal measures the team's productivity and/or the team's contributions to the organization's objectives, whereas in Model #2 all critical elements measure individual performance, with at least one critical element addressing the individual's contribution to the team. Model #3 differs from Model #4 in that the Model #3 approach uses performance appraisals and assigns ratings to individuals; the Model #4 approach does not appraise individual performance and does not assign ratings.

Objective. Since Model #3 places the focus of evaluating performance at the team level rather than at the individual level, management's objective for adopting this approach would be to promote and reward team performance in order to improve organizational effectiveness.

Description

Characteristics

Critical Elements. In a Model #3 approach, at least one, and possibly all, critical elements in an individual's work plan and performance appraisal are based on team or organizational effectiveness/productivity measures. For example, when using a Model #3 approach, an appraisal of an employee who is working in a team setting would have at least one critical element which would depend on the team's performance: did the team meet or exceed its goals?; did the team meet or exceed production levels?; or did the team meet or exceed quality requirements? The rating of the team element(s) is then factored into the rating of the individual.

Significant Difference. The inclusion of a team performance measure in an individual performance appraisal marks the most significant difference between the first two models of this typology and Model #3. In fact, this is the distinguishing factor: Model #3 contains element(s) which specifically measure team performance and Models #1 and #2 do not.

Internal Group Process Measures. In addition to the other measures mentioned in the overview, this model may include internal group process measures. Many consultant firms and authors have developed methods of rating teams on the effectiveness of their internal group processes. Many of these methods include rating forms to be completed by team members and group leaders (Blanchard, Carew and Carew, 1990; Starcevich and Stowell, 1990). These methods attempt to measure processes such as group empowerment, relationships and communication, group flexibility, productivity, recognition and appreciation, and morale. They also measure the effectiveness of the group's structure, its direction, atmosphere and leadership. All these measures taken together supply information on how well the team members work together.

Examples[1]

Aviation Supply Office (ASO), Philadelphia, PA. ASO has developed an appraisal process for its PMRS management team that factors organization performance into the individual managers' performance ratings. All members of the management team have the same work plan elements that focus on customer satisfaction and quality improvement. At the end of the rating period, management team members provide a report of their accomplishment on each work plan element to higher-level management which then rates each individual's performance. At this point, the organization's performance rating is determined by top management and factored into the team members' individual ratings. The rule of determining the final individual rating of record is that no team member's rating can exceed the rating of the organization. In the past three years that this process has been in place, almost all GMs have received the same performance appraisal rating (NPRDC, 1992).

- **Comments of Participants about ASO Appraisal Process**. The satisfaction level with this process is high. The managers who receive their ratings through the ASO process agree that this system is more fair than the previous one and that it encourages movement toward the corporate strategies. There is less competition among team members and teamwork is promoted. There was no team member who wanted to go back to the old system.

New Zealand. New Zealand has passed a law requiring departmental chief executives (the management team) to enter a five-year performance contract (with annual performance reviews) which heavily ties the performance of the department to the rating of the Chief Executive (Boston, 1992). Critical elements are a combination of organizational performance measures and individual performance measures; however, the emphasis and weight of importance in

---

[1] In the research done for this report, there was no organization found that used an individual appraisal system which appraised and rated individuals only on how the team performed (using all critical elements to measure team performance, with no individual elements.)

determining the final rating is placed on organizational performance. Below are additional characteristics of the New Zealand system:

- **Corporate Plan**. Performance agreements must be based on, and consistent with, the relevant department's corporate plan, but they also include an element measuring the personal contribution of the chief executive.

- **Poor Performance**. Poor performance can result in non-renewal or termination of an employment contract.

- **Sources of Input**. Assessments include self appraisal, staff appraisal, and supervisor appraisal. Staff appraisal includes organization performance measurements taken from various data bases (i.e. financial statements, budget accounting, etc.)

- **Accountability**. From evidence gathered, the new system appears to be satisfactory to the parties involved and to have enhanced the accountability of chief executives.

Metropolitan Life Insurance Co. (MetLife). MetLife is using an appraisal approach which meets the definition of Model #3. MetLife performance appraisals have three sections which are used to rate every employee: a corporate section with corporate objectives, a unit or team section with unit/team objectives, and an individual section with individual objectives.

- **Linking Pay to Performance**. For determining rewards for hourly employees, the individual section in MetLife appraisals receives the highest weight, with the unit/team section the next highest, and the corporate section given the least weight. For higher level managers and executives, more weight is given to unit or corporate performance.

Motorola. Motorola has two separate appraisal systems. The individual performance appraisal is called the Performance and Career Planning form and is used for individual career development and for identifying performance problems. The other appraisal system is called an incentive package and contains a formula for determining individual awards that factors team and division performance into the individual's rating and reward determination. It is Motorola's incentive package that resembles a Model #3 approach to performance management as follows:

- **Rewards**. While the career planning appraisal is focused on the individual, the incentive package uses individual, team **and** organization factors. The formula used for determining individual ratings and rewards is: Total Reward is equal to one third of allowed percent for Individual Goals Met plus one third of allowed percent for Team Goals Met plus one third of allowed percent for Division goals met.

Navy Personnel Research and Development Center (NPRDC). Scientists at NPRDC have developed a performance management and team evaluation approach called "Team Oriented

Performance Management" (TOPM) (NPDRC, 1990). TOPM is proposed as a method of performance management in total quality organizations which use teams to accomplish the work. Some of the main features of the TOPM model of appraisal are as follows:

- Individual ratings would be determined using a combination of individual and team elements factored into a formula. The formula proposed is: Individual Performance Appraisal Rating   Process Quality Improvement Score (the team productivity measure) + Team Contribution Score (how well the employee contributed to the team) + Individual Development Score (how the employee has improved his or her process improvement skills.)

- At least three different sources of information would be used to gather the data for the rating process: peer appraisal, supervisory appraisal, and team process performance data gathered from the organization's information system.

- Team goals which directly support organization goals are the focus of appraisal and rewards; individual elements are used only for individual developmental purposes and to comply with the law (5 U.S.C. Chapter 43).

- Feedback on performance to employees is a continuous process through the TQM group structure of the Executive Steering Group, Quality Management Boards, and Process Action Teams. Feedback and appraisal are not just annual events.

- Rewarding team performance over individual performance is emphasized, with productivity gainsharing as the most compatible reward system.

- Using both peer appraisal and supervisory appraisal for determining the team contribution rating is recommended.

- Ratings should be as objective as possible.

- NPRDC encourages activities and/or agencies interested in pursuing this innovative proposal to contact them. The NPRDC staff wish to assist qualifying organizations (both DOD and non-DOD) that are interested in TOPM implementation.

Gateway 2000. In 1989, the U.S. Army's Troop Support Command and Aviation Systems Command submitted a proposal to OPM to establish a demonstration project which they called Gateway 2000 (Hay Group, 1989). Because several problems with the proposal were never resolved to OPM's satisfaction, Gateway 2000 was never implemented. However, the performance management portion of the proposal is worthy of mention as an example of a Model #3 approach to team evaluation.

- Gateway 2000 proposed to include an organizational measure, a unit or team measure, and an individual measure in the final determination of individual appraisal ratings. The formula proposed was: Individual rating = Division score + Team or Unit score + Individual score.

- The formula described above used weighted measures for different types of work. For example, thirty percent of a unit manager's or team leader's rating was based on the Division score, 60 percent on the unit's or team's score, and ten percent on the individual score, whereas only ten percent of a senior clerk's rating would be based on the Division score, with thirty percent on the unit or team's score, and forty percent on the individual score.

- A bonus system was proposed to accompany the performance management system which would have established a threshold payment and target payment, with progressive payout (ranging from the threshold to the target) depending on the performance rating.

DLA Projects. The DLA Ogden Defense Depot and the Memphis site of the Defense Distribution Region Central had in the past proposed new performance appraisal systems similar to the TOPM model developed by NPRDC. The Ogden proposal was canceled because of a change in management philosophy, and the Memphis project was canceled due to labor-relations reasons. (Both proposed systems used organizational and team elements combined with individual performance elements to rate employee performance.)

Analysis

Research Findings

Interdependent Work. Any evaluation system that links team or organizational performance to individual performance appraisals will only be successful in a team environment where most of the work is interdependent (Lawler, 1990; Bartol, 1992; Schuster and Zingheim, 1992).

Combining Individual and Team Measures. Many authors have stated that it is beneficial to combine individual and team measures in appraisal systems. For example, Thornburg wrote:

> "Today's management experts focus on the creation of teamwork and group initiative and performance. Excellence depends on a culture of cross-company cooperation and identification with the purposes of the larger organization. Thus, tomorrow's measures of performance will be increasingly work group-focused...but the individual still has to resolve to work in the group, so there is still room for individual measurement and motivation." (Thornburg, 1991)

Promoting Organizational Performance. One of the central purposes of factoring team performance into individual performance appraisals is to establish and promote the importance of meeting group goals which will foster the improvement of organization performance. In The New Pay: Linking Employee and Organizational Performance, Jay R. Schuster and Patricia K.

Zingheim outlined the importance of bringing an organization's goals into the forefront of the appraisal and reward system. They wrote:

> "It is more difficult and time-consuming to set goals and standards for individual jobs than for groups...Individual standards also generally receive less scrutiny and hence have less consistency in quality than performance standards set for groups. Because group performance requires a more macro focus than individual performance, group performance goals are more likely to be consistent with the organization's direction." (Schuster and Zingheim, 1992).

Using Team Performance Measures for Evaluation. Edward E. Lawler supports the concept of using team performance measures to appraise performance and reward individuals. In his book Strategic Pay: Aligning Organizational Strategies and Pay Systems, Mr. Lawler advises organizations that it is a mistake to design work for groups and then ask supervisors to appraise the performance of individuals. He states:

> "Individual appraisal makes sense with such individual tasks as selling certain products, offering legal services, and producing simple products, but it does not fit selling complex computer systems, settling complex legal cases, or manufacturing many high-technology products (Schuster, 1984; Von Glinow and Mohrman, 1989).In the latter cases, teams of individuals need to perform well, and as a result good performance measures exist only at the team level." (Lawler, 1990, page 92).

Advantages of Using Model #3 (Group Performance Element)

Promotes Teamwork. Model #3 encourages, promotes and supports teamwork and team and/or organization performance.

Less Internal Competition. Model #3 attempts to eliminate internal competition between individuals.

Focus on Organization's Goals. Because team performance is factored into the individual's appraisal, this approach places the focus of performance on a larger scale and is more directly linked to the organization's goals.

TQM. Model #3 supports TQM, employee involvement and high-performance initiatives.

An Investment. Model #3 is a strategic, long-term investment in organizational performance improvement efforts.

Can Improve Productivity. Under the right conditions and in the correct environment, it can improve productivity and quality.

Disadvantages of Using Model #3

Costs. Using a Model #3 approach may cause significant short-term start-up costs.

Time. A Model #3 approach takes time to phase in.

Employee Attitudes. If employees have not been involved and trained properly, individuals may resent being assigned a team rating. This could be a significant problem with those who have normally received outstanding ratings based on their personal work performance and who are perceived to be the "stars."

Measures. Performance measures may be more complex than measures used in Models #1 and #2, especially for service and nonproduction jobs.

Using Team Measures ONLY. If **only** team or organization measures are used to rate employees (with no individual measures): (a) performance problems may not be addressed adequately; (b) consideration of performance in RIF determinations could not be made on an individual level; (c) individual development plans would have to be addressed using a mechanism other than performance appraisal; and (d) an alternate method would have to be used to determine promotion potential based on individual performance.

Performance-Based Actions. Sustaining performance-based actions before the Merit Systems Protection Board (under 5 U.S.C. Chapter 43) would be questionable. Currently, no action has been appealed that was based on a rating that included team performance measures.

Optimum Organizational Environment

Interdependent Work. An interdependent work environment such as that found in organizations extensively using employee involvement programs and/or teams, is required.

Top Management Support. The use of the Model #3 approach must be part of an overall strategic plan to improve organizational performance and must be completely supported and promoted by top management.

Support Cooperation. The values of the organization must focus on teamwork and group performance. The climate must support cooperation rather than competition.

TQM Environment. An organization which has implemented TQM would be suitable for using Model #3.

Other Criteria. NPRDC has developed a list of organization selection criteria for implementing their TOPM model (NPRDC, 1990). Most of the criteria would apply to any organization that wishes to take a Model #3 approach to team evaluation. Criteria identified by NPRDC which should be found in an organization prior to adopting a Model #3 approach (and which have not been mentioned above) are as follows. The organization should:

- have a published philosophy, vision statement, and/or mission statement.

- have, or should be able to develop, identifiable process measures without great difficulty.

- have good labor/management relations.

- should be willing to undertake major organizational changes.

- have a training plan for delivering training on the performance management system to all employees and teams. For best success, employees need to be involved as soon as possible.

- have identified their external customers and should have begun developing feedback mechanisms.

- have a willingness to collect measures of all kinds and make decisions based on the data.

- have a trusting, cooperative, and communicative workplace.

- have some kind of ongoing employee involvement system.

Cost Factors

Design and Implementation. The costs of designing a new system and implementation may be higher in this model than in the first two models of the continuum (i.e., training, developing evaluation measures which might require computerized data bases, manpower costs used to plan implementation, etc.)

Ongoing costs will be incurred such as continued training, maintenance of computerized information system, etc.

Summary/Comments

Summary. The Model #3 approach represents an attempt to link team performance to individual performance by factoring the team's performance into the individual's performance rating. This is done by having at least one element (possibly all) of the individual's appraisal involve measurement of team performance, i.e. did the team meet its goals? did the team produce a quality product? does the team work well together? This approach may be used by organizations that use teamwork to accomplish a significant portion of the work, that have well-developed teams, or that for whatever reason want to enhance teamwork.

Comments. Many authors, consultants and managers feel that the time has come to recognize interdependence in the workplace. As work in many organizations becomes more technical and complex, employees are increasingly dependent upon each other to accomplish their work. Instantaneous communication worldwide has both fostered and facilitated interdependence. Private industry has been in the forefront among organizations in acknowledging the interdependence of employees, organizing employees into teams to maximize productivity, and recognizing the importance of team contributions to the achievement of organizational objectives. Federal agencies have also begun to recognize the importance of interdependence in the workplace, as evidenced by the fact that a high percentage of agencies are now using teams as part of their TQM efforts to improve quality, productivity, and customer satisfaction. However, though there has been widespread recognition of the value of teams and team performance, performance measures in the Federal sector have remained largely individual performance measures. Model #3 offers a valuable approach for focusing on and measuring team performance. Using team performance measures fosters cooperation rather than competition in the workplace and supports the accomplishment of team and organizational objectives. While the development of team performance measures requires an initial investment of time and money, the expense is worthwhile, as team measures are a long-term investment in an organization's efforts to improve quality, productivity, and customer satisfaction.

MODEL #4
No Individual Performance Appraisal

Introduction

Definition. Model #4 focuses exclusively on team or organizational performance and assumes no individual performance appraisal. The foremost proponent of this theory is W. Edwards Deming who believes that any type of appraisal fosters unhealthy competition and reduces morale.

Place On the Continuum. Model #4 is at the far end of the focus continuum in that this approach focuses only on team or organizational performance, completely eliminating individual performance appraisal altogether. Model #3 differs from Model #4 in that Model #3 uses a performance planning and assessment system that involves individual and team performance elements, while Model #4 assigns no ratings to individuals. Performance feedback to teams is given through productivity or quality measures denoting variations in the process being performed (e.g., how long it takes on average to perform the process), not variations in individual performance.

Objective. The objective of using Model #4 is to eliminate the negative impacts of individual appraisal and to concentrate instead on improving the performance of the organization. In practice, the few organizations that have approached this model have used variations, since the theoretical model is difficult to institute in any organization due to the lack of any linkage to other personnel actions. The Model #4 approach cannot be used in Federal agencies (unless implemented as part of a demonstration project) because it does not meet existing Federal legal requirements.

Description

Characteristics

No Individual Appraisal. Theoretically, no appraisal, individual or group, should be done at all. In practice, common model variations provide for the establishment of organizational "control limits" (with the vast majority of employees falling inside the limits), or require that all individuals working in the group (organization and/or team) receive the same appraisal.

Quality Problems. An underlying philosophy is that most quality problems are management's responsibility and that management can provide the means by which workers can continuously improve by instituting such mechanisms as statistical process controls (SPCs) and the formation of work teams.

Statistical Process Controls (SPCs). SPCs are parameters which define system variation or the boundaries for the "normal" work range (i.e., what range is considered acceptable in the processes that occur each time a product is made or service is carried out.) However, these controls are not used as a policing or valuative device for individual performance. By analyzing instances in which a measurement point is "out of control", one can assess in what area(s) changes need to be made (e.g., employee, methods, tools.)

Control Charts. Ideally, employees are trained in simple statistical analyses that help them chart their performance, producing "control charts" for work processes. Employees then take samples of their work processes over time and compute an average.

Poor Performance. Attention is directed toward those people who consistently perform outside (above or below) the SPC limits. However, for employees falling below the SPC "acceptable" range, training and/or peer pressure from the team members is/are the expected remedies to bring an employee's work back within the limits.

Team Work. The team configuration assumes that workers will be involved in planning their work and solving quality problems.

Rewards. Theories on the use of rewards with a Model #4 approach differ considerably by organization. The following are a few examples:

- If rewards are given, all employees should receive the same reward.

- No one should be rewarded or punished, and salary increases should be based on factors other than performance, e.g., seniority, market rate, and the company's productivity or prosperity (e.g., gainsharing) etc.

- Only those employees whose performance is outside (above) the SPC parameters should be rewarded.

Examples

PACER SHARE. This Federal Government demonstration project at the Directorate of Distribution of the Sacramento Air Logistics Center located at McClellan Air Force Base, California, was initiated to test a more flexible and streamlined personnel system and new ways of motivating employees to improve the organization's performance. Beginning in February 1988, evaluation of employees' individual performance for the purposes of giving performance ratings ceased. (However, since there were still situations in which employees needed to interface with other Federal agencies, employees retained ratings in their official files. The "interface" performance ratings for PACER SHARE employees were determined by averaging the ratings of all employees within the McClellan AFB competitive area. The averages were calculated for the combination of pay grades that were equivalent to the paybands used in PACER SHARE. Employees entering the project with ratings higher than the calculated average, retained the higher rating for merit promotion consideration.) Major components of the PACER SHARE project are described below:

- **Pay Banding**. In this demonstration project, the traditional grades and steps were replaced by pay bands. Progression within bands was based on longevity only; competitive promotions between pay bands were based on qualifications, as opposed to time in pay level. Base pay increments were tied either to annual "white collar" General Schedule increases or "blue collar" local wage indexes. Process improvement and monitoring devices against which organizational performance would be measured were supposed to replace individual-focused appraisals but were never fully developed.

- **Job Proficiency Guide (JPG)**. This was developed more or less as a replacement for job standards. It set forth individual job requirements (knowledge and skills necessary for each employee to possess in order to perform their job successfully.) Training was centered around the contents of the JPG and completion of the JPG meant an employee was considered to be proficient in that position.

- **Poor Performance**. In those cases where peer influence/training was not instrumental in raising an employee's productivity to the "acceptable range," one of the negotiated Demonstration Project regulations provided for a step-by-step procedure to identify, validate and resolve individual employee performance problems within the Project by considering alternate solutions. This was to be accomplished by an investigative review by a labor/management team and a labor/management review board reaching a decision by consensus.

- **Gainsharing**. PACER SHARE included a productivity gainsharing program which provided performance awards on an organization-wide level. All members of an organization shared in the rewards for improved organizational performance. A productivity gainsharing formula was used to estimate cost savings; one half of the savings was returned to the Government and the other half was divided among the organization's employees. Evaluations of the project were conducted, but numerous organizational alignments and organizational downsizings made it difficult to fully track the impact of the project. The demonstration project ended in February 1993 upon the expiration of its authorized term.

General Motors Powertrain Division. In 1989, this organization replaced its six-tiered appraisal system with one that uses no individual ratings. A statistical study of the old system showed that seventy-five percent of sixteen hundred covered employees were in the top two categories. It was determined that without a forced distribution, ratings systems would always become top-heavy over time. Their current system is described below:

- **Employee Development**. The personal development system in place today in the Powertrain Division is based on the belief that the only justification for performance appraisals is to help people develop. The system has been expanded to cover eight thousand salaried employees in twenty-twp organizations. Among other features, it eliminates ratings and separates compensation decisions from appraisals. Outstanding employees, of which there were only four in 1989 and only a handful each year since, are identified and rewarded outside the appraisal system. Under the personal development system, employees and supervisors meet at the beginning of the year and agree on job responsibilities, priorities, opportunities, and training needs. Feedback from mutually selected employees and customers is also solicited. At the final meeting, the supervisor and employee discuss all sources of feedback in developing the next year's plan.

US West. In 1992, individual appraisals were abolished at US West Communications' Home and Personal Services Market Unit. This division of over four thousand Union employees is responsible for telemarketing, credit and collections, and sales. On average, thirty million calls per year are handled, serving customers in a fourteen-state territory. Listed below are some characteristics of their performance management system (old and new):

- **The Old System**. Under the old US West system, performance measurements were internally focused (i.e., number of calls per hour, length of time on call, sales quotas, "hitting the numbers.") Management and employees alike felt that the appraisal system encouraged overaggressive sales practices and produced questionable behaviors that were driven by unrealistic quotas.

- **Partnership**. In response to employee survey results that showed low employee morale and job satisfaction, US West management, employees and labor representatives felt that a change in culture was needed. They entered into a partnership that emphasizes customer focus, trust between labor and management, teams, and worker autonomy.

- **Team-Based**. The new US West system is team-based and focuses on mutually-developed team goals. Employees individually collect their own performance data and share it with team members and their coach(es). Additional input from customers, coaches and team members is received and discussed.

- **Coaching**. Employees are coached to desired behavior rather than numbers. The desired behaviors are adapted to the operating strategies of the market unit to insure congruity and alignment, and have been communicated to all employees.

- **Poor Performance**. Low contributors are encouraged toward better performance through personalized coaching, the team process and peer influence (e.g., failure to handle fair share of calls forces a heavier workload on colleagues). If a low contributor is identified, the coach helps the employee develop an individualized plan of improvement.

- **Employee Surveys**. An Employee Satisfaction Survey and Culture Progress Questionnaire were developed to evaluate the new system's success. Responses to the surveys indicate widespread satisfaction and acceptance of the new system. Operating results have remained stable and shown improvement in some areas.

A Department of Energy Group Bonus Program. Currently, unless exempted from performance appraisal provisions of the law (5 U.S.C. Chapter 43), agencies are required to provide employees with individual, annual appraisals. In keeping with their participative, team-oriented cultures, however, some organizations de-link their awards programs from any measure of individual performance. At the Department of Energy's Richland Operations Office, the Group Bonus Program bases individual General Schedule (GS) awards solely on organizational performance. No GS individual performance awards or Quality Step Increases are given. Employees have to receive Fully Successful performance ratings in order to be eligible for the group awards, and divisions within the organization can receive different dollar amounts based on the division's attainment of organizational goals.

Analysis

Research Findings

Few Examples. While much is publicized about the Deming approach, little in the way of actual implementation has occurred so that it is difficult to fully assess this approach.

Quality Initiatives. The concept of eliminating performance appraisal is most often presented as one facet of an overall quality approach. The quality approach comes out of a human resources model which commonly assumes that work is intrinsically satisfying to employees and that, given the opportunity, people want to participate in planning their work and can be given responsibility. While these assumptions accurately describe many employees, they may not hold up for all, or even the majority of, employees in an organization.

Elaboration on Deming's Teachings (Joiner Associates Inc.). Peter Scholtes of Joiner Associates Inc. is a principal proponent of the Deming philosophy and has written on ways to make the model operational. Some of Mr. Scholtes' suggestions for creating alternative appraisal systems are:

- **Regular Feedback.** In place of ratings, provide regular feedback to employees through development of lists of major feedback resources, e.g., peers, customers, suppliers, etc., and an agenda and method for obtaining feedback.

- **Salary**. Link salaries and bonuses to such things as market rate, accumulation of skills, increased responsibilities, seniority, and/or prosperity of the whole organization.

- **Promotion**. Identify candidates for promotion through such means as designing special assignments that contain elements of the promotion job, observing the candidate in specially designed activities, involving the customer in developing the methods and/or criteria for selection, and/or developing an organizational culture that is less dependent on promotions.

- **Communication**. Instead of using performance to give direction, managers should develop and communicate the organization's mission and operating philosophy, spend extensive time with employees in planning sessions, and communicate with subordinates and superiors on a consistent basis. General communication is promoted by meetings, focus or feedback groups, and/or walking around and listening, observing and talking to workers.

- **Training Needs Assessment**. Assess an employee's need for training by, first, accurately defining job requirements so that designed training and educational experiences can address job needs. Then, communication during informal contacts can identify and explore training opportunities. Underlying this approach is a commitment to comprehensive on-going training and education for all employees.

PMRS Review Committee Report Model. As part of the background for the PMRS Review Committee's report (November, 1991), each member proposed possible models for a new PMRS system. One of the models outlines the general concepts of the Deming philosophy. The basic characteristics of this system are:

- There are no performance ratings.

- Group performance, not individual performance, is emphasized.

- Feedback replaces ratings.

- The manager and employee jointly set goals.

- All employees get the same base pay and cash award amounts.

- Individuals may receive special act awards and/or awards from gainsharing programs.

- Peer pressure is relied on for motivation of team members.

Not Compatible. The report does not, nor is its purpose to, flesh out details of any of the models presented. Moreover, no one model in its entirety is recommended for a new system. Also, it should be noted that the PMRS Review Committee did not consider this Deming-like approach to be particularly compatible with the Government's environment and expectations concerning the need for assessing individual employee performance and accountability.

Alternatives to Current Personnel Program Requirements. As explained in the overview of this report, Model #4 does not meet current requirements for performance appraisal. It would also require changes in other personnel programs. Below are some alternative approaches to the procedures of other personnel programs in a Model #4 environment. (Many of the alternative approaches listed below could be used **in addition to** the approaches currently in use, especially in organizations that use quality management practices.)

- **When Official Performance Ratings are Needed**. As mentioned earlier, the PACER/SHARE demonstration project acknowledged that employees needed "official ratings" when interfacing with agencies having traditional appraisal systems. For those times, each employee retained an "official rating" that was negotiated between union and management.

- **Poor Performance**. Deming suggests that poor performers have an identifiable problem, such as an inability to learn the job. He says that since the organization hired the employee, it has a "moral" obligation to put him/her in the right job. He places the responsibility on making the employee productive on the organization. (Note: Deming's approach does not meet current legal requirements in the Federal Government for dealing with unacceptable performance.) If an employee won't work, then the problem is disciplinary, not performance-related, and appropriate action should be taken.

- **Promotion**. Scholtes suggests that other factors could be used to identify candidates for promotion. These factors include: special assignments that contain elements of the promotion job or "customer" involvement in developing criteria and in the selection process.

- **Employee Development**. Scholtes says that all training should be based on the job and its requirements. By accurately defining job requirements, methods to determine employees' capabilities for each of the necessary competencies can be designed. Training would be based on the needs of the employee.

Advantages of Using Model #4 (No Individual Appraisal)

No Appraisals. Eliminating performance appraisal entirely (or at least individual appraisal) helps:

- reduce unhealthy competition and/or fear among workers in an organization.

- focus the organization more on long-term goals.

- provide a better balance between quality and quantity, since "managing by numbers" tends to emphasize quantity.

- reduces possible artificial distinctions among employees, especially when variation is related more to the system than to the workers.

- eliminate an administrative function seen by many as a waste of time.

41

Teamwork. Promoting teamwork encourages stronger working relationships and better communication among employees.

Disadvantages of Using Model #4

Implementation. Implementing this model appears to take much initial preparation of the workforce in terms of clarifying the philosophy on which the model is based, training people to work in teams, training people in feedback techniques, analyzing the work to outline team tasks and/or organizational productivity measures, and defining linkages to other personnel systems, e.g., promotion, discipline, awards, etc.

No Individual Recognition. While a main advantage may be reduced competition among individuals, individuals may also miss the acknowledgement that, for some, helps bolster self esteem and productivity. It has also been found that most Federal workers (sixty-nine percent) prefer that their ratings be based on individual performance (OPM, 1992), leading to the conclusion that a total team approach goes against the traditional American outlook of "rugged individualism".

No Rating to Link to Other Personnel Actions. Lack of individual appraisals creates a less solid basis for traditionally linked personnel actions, such as removals, awards, promotions, and disciplinary actions.

Optimum Organizational Environment

Similar to Model #3. The optimum organizational characteristics listed under this section for Model #3 apply to Model #4 as well.

Type of Work. SPCs can be more easily developed in a "blue collar", as opposed to a "white collar", work environment since the former setting has more visible, product-oriented outcomes that are more conducive to quantifiable measurement.

Interdependent Work. The more employee tasks are naturally interdependent and create a final product based on the combination of all the tasks, the easier it is to justify the elimination of all ratings or individual ratings.

A Team Environment. The Deming model, or variations of it, would appear to work best in organizations in which the employees work in defined groups or teams. A hallmark of both the theoretical and more practical approaches of this model emphasize team involvement in planning, monitoring, and receipt of rewards. Therefore, job tasks that are interdependent and organizations in which defined and active communication channels have been set up would fare better with this approach.

Cost Factors

Initial Costs. Initial costs are high for developing SPCs and training managers and employees in the philosophy and processes of the new system.

Production Time Lengthened Initially. Particularly in the initial stages of instituting this model, production time may be lengthened since employees need to learn a new measurement system (i.e., how to chart their progress against developed SPCs.) In general, team input into planning and involvement in problem solving normally may take longer than if unilateral decisions are made by upper management; however, it is expected that production would increase overall in the long run.

Training Costs. Since emphasis on employee development is high, ongoing coaching and formal and informal training expenditures will be required.

Skills. Communication skills of all workers need to be initially enhanced and maintained to make the team concept viable; therefore, costs associated with ongoing training in communication skills, possibly supplemented by group facilitators, may be required.

Summary/Comments

Summary. Model #4 represents a completely organization-focused approach to performance planning and assessment as was practiced in the PACER\SHARE demonstration project at McClellan Air Force Base in California and as is promoted by Dr. W. Edwards Deming. This model lies at the end of the focus continuum with only the organization's performance evaluated. At this point on the continuum, there are no individual appraisals done or ratings given. Organizations interested in using this model should have a highly developed systematic measurement system in place, should have other mechanisms for employee feedback and development, and must have a high-performance culture to consider adopting this approach. Currently, Federal agencies cannot adopt this model unless it is part of a demonstration project.

Comments. The philosophy of Model #4 is hard to implement in its purest sense. Most examples of Model #4 use variations of its basic principles. An important feature of this model is its emphasis on employee involvement in planning, peer assistance, and ongoing problem solving. These practices can enhance any working environment and be incorporated into most organizations regardless of the basic appraisal model used. Finally, Model #4, both in theory and in its variations, will be better assessable as more organizations experiment with its concepts.

Appendix 1

ANNOUNCEMENT OF THE
IAG PERFORMANCE MANAGEMENT WORKING GROUP ON
EVALUATING TEAM PERFORMANCE

BACKGROUND:

-Traditionally, the focus of performance appraisal and actions resulting from it has been on the individual. This has been particularly true in government, where measures of organizational performance based on profit/loss are not feasible.

-Employees often work in teams, either formally or informally, permanently or temporarily. "Quality Circle"-type projects, "Employee Involvement" efforts and TQM initiatives tend to emphasize teamwork, cooperation and group achievement over individual performance.

-While law and regulation applicable to federal employees mention organizational performance and presumably permit its consideration in the appraisal process, experience shows that most federal employee performance appraisals are based entirely on individual performance.

ISSUES:

-Should organizational performance, particularly that of a team/work group be part of the appraisal?

-If YES:

-A major part, the only part?

-Can team performance be effectively measured? How?

-What are the appropriate sources of appraisal input? Supervisors, other team members/peers, customers?

-What are appropriate actions which could result from the appraisal; e.g. awards, pay raises, alternate forms of recognition, negative actions? Would this approach negate the traditional authority of the supervisor to take or initiate these actions?

-What is possible impact on individual achievement?

CONTACTS:
Gary McLean, FCC (202) 632-7541
David Orr, FEC (202) 219-4290

Members of the Working Group on Evaluating Team Performance

David S. Orr
Federal Election Commission
999 E St., NW., Room 812
Washington, DC 20463
Ph. (202) 219-4290

Kim Green
Department of Labor
Office of Employment&Eval.
200 Constitution Ave. NW Rm. N5470
Washington, DC 20210
Ph. (202) 219-6525

Evelyn Guerra
Department of Energy
1000 Independence Ave., SW
Rm. 4F051
Washington, DC 20585
Ph. (202) 586-9963

Efstathia Siegel and
Karen Lebing, OPM,
1900 E Street, NW., Rm. 7454
Washington, DC 20415
Ph. (202) 606-2720

Dennis McGowan and
Maribeth Zankowski
AID, FA/HRDM/PPM
2401 E St., NW
Rm. 1130, SA #1
Washington, DC 20523
Ph. (202) 663-1433

Gary McLean
FCC-Office of Human Resources
1919 M St., NW
Washington, DC 20554
Ph. (202) 632-7541

John McGrath
GAO, Office of Personnel
441 G Street, NW., Rm. 1318
Washington, DC 20548
Ph. (202) 512-7657

Janis Nash
U.S. Geological Survey
215 National Center
12201 Sunrise Valley Dr.
Reston, VA 22092
Ph. (703) 648-7423

Janis Seelig
Nat'l Labor Relations Board
1717 Pennsylvania Ave.
Rm. 334
Washington, DC 20570
Ph. (202) 254-9080 or 273-3900

Janice Smith
Department of Commerce
Office of HRM
14th&Constitution Ave., NW, Rm. 5108
Washington, DC 20230
Ph. (202) 482-4861

**Denis Pelley, Syrena West,
Dick Boylston, Dorene White,**
and **Phil Seneschal**
Headquarters USAF/DPCK
1040 Air Force Pentagon
Washington, DC 20330-1040
Ph. (703) 695-9106

Appendix 3

CONTACTS

Pat Moylan
Defense Management Engineering College (DMEC)
(formerly Army Management Engineering College (AMEC))
Rock Island, Illinois
Phone: (309) 782-0888 or (309) 782-0450

Marvin Sandler
Aviation Supply Office (ASO)
Philadelphia, Pennsylvania
Phone: (215) 697-1375

Dr. Del Nebeker
Navy Personnel Research and Development Center (NPRDC)
San Diego, California
Phone: (619) 553-7979

Dr. Michael White
Navy Personnel Research and Development Center (NPRDC)
San Diego, California
Phone: (619) 553-7954

Peter Scholtes
Joiner Associates
Madison, Wisconsin
Phone: (608) 238-8134

BIBLIOGRAPHY

Codes: "O"= Applicable to the Overview and all models
                     "1"= Applicable to Model #1
                     "2"= Applicable to Model #2
                     "3"= Applicable to Model #3
                     "4"= Applicable to Model #4

<u>Code</u>

O   Bartol, Kathryn M. and Laura L. Hagmann, "Team-Based Pay Plans: A Key to Effective Teamwork", **Compensation & Benefits Review**, November-December 1992, pages 24-29.

O   Beck, David, "Implementing a Gainsharing Plan: What Companies Need to Know", **Compensation & Benefits Review**, January-February, 1992. pages 21-33.

O   Benson, Tracy E., "Quality and Teamwork", **Industry Week**, April 6, 1992, pages 66-68.

O   Berson-Besthoff, Paige and Charles Peck, "Small Group Incentives: Goal-Based Pay", Report Number 1006, New York, NY: The Conference Board, 1992.

3   Blanchard, Kenneth, Donald Carew and Eunice Parisi-Carew, <u>The One Minute Manager Builds High Performing Teams,</u> New York, NY: William Morrow and Company, 1990.

3   Boston, Jonathan, "Assessing the Performance of Departmental Chief Executives: Perspectives from New Zealand", **Public Administration**, Vol 70 Autumn 1992, pages 405-428.

O   Boyett, Joseph H. and Henry P. Conn, <u>Workplace 2000</u>, New York, NY: Dutton, 1991.

O   Comola, Jackie P., Designing a New Family of Measures, In: (Eds.) Schein, L. & Berman, M. A., <u>Total Quality Performance: Highlights of a Conference,</u> Washington, DC: The Conference Board, Inc., 1988.

O   "Computer Companies Ambitiously Remake Quality Improvement Efforts", **Productivity**, October 1992, pages 1-3.

O   "Crew Award Program Proposal", Bonneville Power Administration, July, 1992.

O   Cumming, Charles M., "Will Traditional Salary Administration Survive the Stampede to Alternative Rewards?" <u>Compensation & Benefits Review</u>, Nov-Dec 1992, pages 42-47.

4   Deming, W. Edwards, <u>Quality, Productivity and Competitive Position</u>, Cambridge, MA: Massachusetts Institute of Technology, Center for Advanced Engineering Study, 1982.

O   Doyle, Robert J., <u>Gainsharing and Productivity: A Guide to Planning, Implementation, and Development</u>, New York, NY: AMACOM Book Division, 1983.

O   Duke, Lois Lovelace, "Greenville, SC and Alexandria, VA: Problems and Successes Using Private Sector Techniques to Motivate Personnel in the Public Sector", **Public Personnel Management**, Vol 18 No. 4, Winter 1989, pages 440-456.

O   Eccles, Robert G., "The Performance Measurement Manifesto", **Harvard Business Review**, January-February 1991, pages 131-137.

O   Edman, Donald H., "Compensation for the 1990s: A Look at IBM", **Compensation and Benefits Review**, 1991. pages 32-39.

3   Ege, Roger, "Group Performance Appraisal System" and other documents received from Defense Logistics Agency, Defense Depot Ogden. 1991.

O   Epstein, Paul D. "Measuring the Performance of Public Services" <u>Public Productivity Handbook</u> ed by Marc Holzer, New York, NY: Marcel Dekker Inc. 1992.

O   Financial Management Service, Department of the Treasury, "Project USA, Performance Measurement: Report on a Survey of Private Sector Performance Measures", January 1993.

O   Gabris, Gerald T., "Monetary Incentives and Performance: Is there an Administratively Meaningful Connection?", <u>Public Productivity Handbook</u>, Marc Holzer (ed), New York, NY: Marcel Dekker Inc. 1992.

4   General Motors Corp. "Slide Presentation: GM Power Train Apparatus Division (Quality Processes)," Detroit, Michigan: Quality Control Conference, October 1992.

O   Graber, Jim M., Roger E. Breisch and Walter E. Breisch, "Performance Appraisals and Deming: A Misunderstanding?", **Quality Progress**, June 1992. pages 50-62.

O Graham-Moore, Brian E. and Timothy Ross, <u>Productivity Gainsharing: How Employee Incentive Programs can Improve Business Performance</u>, Englewood Cliffs, NJ: Prentice Hall Inc., 1983.

3 Green, John, "Teamwork May Revamp Appraisals", **TQM Quarterly**, Defense Logistics Agency, October 1991.

O Halachmi, Arie, "Evaluation Research: Purpose and Perspective", <u>Public Productivity Handbook</u>, ed by Marc Holzer, New York, NY: Marcel Dekker Inc. 1992.

O Hatry, Harry P. and Donald M. Fisk, "Measuring Productivity in the Public Sector", <u>Public Productivity Handbook</u>, ed by Marc Holzer, New York, NY: Marcel Dekker Inc. 1992.

3 Hitchcock, Darcy E. and Marsha Willard, "Measuring Team Progress", **Journal for Quality and Participation**, September 1992. pages 12-18.

O Huge, Ernest C., "Measuring and Rewarding Performance", <u>Total Quality: An Executive's Guide for the 1990s</u>, The Ernst and Young Quality Improvement Consulting Group, Homewood, IL: Business One Irwin, 1990. pages 70-88.

3 Huret, Judy, "Paying for Team Results", **HRMagazine**, May 1991. pages 39-41.

O Imberman, Woodruff, "Boosting Plant Performance with Gainsharing", **Business Horizons**, November-December 1992. pages 77-79.

4 Johnson, E.K., "Total Quality Management and Performance Appraisal: To Be or Not To Be? A Literature Review and Case Studies," U.S. Office of Personnel Management, Research and Demonstration Division, July 1990.

O Johnson, Sam T., "Work Teams: What's Ahead in Work Design and Rewards Management", **Compensation & Benefits Review**, March-April, 1993. pages 35-41.

O Kennedy, Peter W., "Quality Management Challenges Compensation Professionals," **Journal of Compensation and Benefits**, March-April, 1993. pages 29-35.

O LawlerIII, Edward E., <u>Strategic Pay: Aligning Organizational Strategies and Pay Systems</u>, San Francisco: Jossey-Bass Publishers, 1990.

O Levine, Hermine Zagat, "The Board Speaks Out: Compensation and Benefits in the 1990s, Part 1", **Compensation and Benefits Review**,

O   Masternak, Robert L., "Gainsharing Programs at Two Fortune 500 Facilities: Why One Worked Better", **National Productivity Review**, Winter 1991/1992. pages 71-86.

O   Masternak, Robert L. and Timothy L. Ross, "Gainsharing: A Bonus Plan or Employee Involvement?", **Compensation & Benefits Review**, January-February, 1992. pages 46-54.

O   McAdams, Jerry L. and Elizabeth J. Hawk, "Capitalizing on Human Assets: Summary Report", American Compensation Association and Maritz Inc, 1992.

O   McAdams, Jerry L. and Elizabeth J. Hawk, "Performance-Based Rewards...What Works and Why", **Journal of Compensation and Benefits**, March-April, 1993. pages 52-54.

O   McNutt, Robert P., "Sharing Across the Board: Du Pont's Achievement Sharing Program", **Compensation and Benefits Review**, 1991. pages 17-24.

4   Navy Personnel Research and Development Center, "Pacer Share Summary", January 6, 1993.

3   Navy Personnel Research and Development Center, "Team Oriented Performance Management: A Concept Paper", San Diego, CA, December 1990.

O   Nickel, James E. and Sandra O'Neal, "Small-Group Incentives: Gain Sharing in the Microcosm", **Compensation and Benefits Review**, March-April 1990, pages 22-29.

O   Pay For Performance Labor-Management Committee, "Strengthening the Link Between Pay and Performance: The Report of The Committee", November 1991.

O   Performance Management and Recognition System Review Committee, Advancing Managerial Excellence: A Report on Improving the Performance Management and Recognition System, November 5, 1991.

3   "Performance Sharing Program for 1992", with "Short Term Performance Compensation Plan", Metropolitan Life Insurance Company, 1992.

O   "Policy Initiatives for Position Classification and Performance Management", Classification and Performance Management Working Group, June 10, 1992.

O   Pritchard, Robert D., Measuring and Improving Organizational Productivity: A Practical Guide, New York, NY: Praeger Publishers, 1990.

O   Pritchard, Robert D., Lawrence G. Weiss, Amie Hedley Goode, and Lauri A. Jensen, "Measuring Organizational Productivity with ProMES", **National Productivity Review**, Vol. 9, No. 3/Summer 1990.

3   "Report on a Design for the Compensation System Component of the U.S. Army's Troop Support Command and Aviation Systems Command: Gateway 2000 Demonstration Project", Hay Group, 1989.

4   Scholtes, Peter R., "An Elaboration of Deming's Teaching on Performance Appraisal," Madison, Wisconsin: Joiner Associates, Inc., 1987.

O   Schuster, Jay R. and Patricia K. Zingheim, <u>The New Pay: Linking Employee and Organizational Performance</u>, New York, NY: Lexington Books, 1992.

O   "Small Group Incentives: Goal-Based Pay", Report Number 1006, New York, NY: The Conference Board, Inc., 1992.

3   Starcevich, Matt M. and Steven J. Stowell, <u>Teamwork: We Have Met the Enemy and They are Us</u>, Salt Lake City, Utah: The Center For Management and Organization Effectiveness, 1990.

O   "Synthesis of Groups' Recommendations", from Directors of Personnel Conference entitled "Performance and Classification: Integrating Effective Change", February 7, 1992.

O   Thompson, Brad Lee. "An Early Review of Peer Review", **Training**, July, 1991.

O   Thornburg, Linda, "Performance Measures that Work", **HRMagazine**, May 1991, pages 35-38.

O   Thornburg, Linda, "How Do You Cut the Cake?", **HRMagazine**, October 1992, pages 66-72.

2   U.S. Air Force, "Total Quality (TQ) Elements and Standards for Work Plans", Memorandum to DPC, January 1990.

2   U.S. General Accounting Office, "1992 PFP/APSS Assessment Handbook", Washington, D.C., May 1992.

O   U.S. General Accounting Office, "Federal Performance Management: Agencies Need Greater Flexibility in Designing Their Systems" (GAO/GGD-93-57), February 1993.

O   U.S. General Accounting Office, "Office of Personnel Management: Better Performance Information Needed", (GAO\GGD-90-44), February 1990.

O   U.S. General Accounting Office, "Program Performance Measures: Federal Agency Collection and Use of Performance Data", (GAO\GGD-93-65), May 1992.

O   U.S. General Accounting Office, "Quality Management: Survey of Federal Organizations", (GAO\GGD-93-9BR), October 1992.

O   U.S. Office of Management and Budget, "Memorandum, subj: Financial Statements and Performance Measures", February 5, 1992.

2   U.S. Office of Personnel Management, Federal Personnel Manual System, FPM Bulletin 990-90. "Total Quality Management." Washington, D.C., November 18, 1992.

4   U.S. Office of Personnel Management, "PACER SHARE: A Federal Productivity and Personnel Management Demonstration Project, Fourth-Year Evaluation Report". December 1992.

O   U.S. Office of Personnel Management, "Survey of Federal Employees", Special Report, May 1992.

O   U.S. Office of Personnel Management, Personnel Systems and Oversight Group, Performance Management and Incentive Awards Division. "360 Degree Performance Appraisal: Other Sources of Input for Employee Evaluations (Draft)." Washington, D.C., December 1992.

2   U.S. Office of Personnel Management, San Francisco Regional Office, "Sample Performance Standards for Use in a Total Quality Management Environment," January 1992.

O   Walker, Terry, "Creating Total Quality Improvement That Lasts", **National Productivity Review**, Autumn 1992, pages 173-476.

4   Walton, Mary, Deming Management at Work, New York: G.P. Putnam's Sons, Inc., 1990. pp.225 - 227.

O   "What's the Best Incentive for Employees?" **HR Focus**, May 1992, page 22.

3   White, Michael A. and Amy L. Culbertson, "Recognizing, Awarding, and Appraising People in a Total Quality Leadership Organization: The Naval Aviation Supply Office Model", TQLO Publication No. 92-04, December 1992.

O   Wholey, Joseph S. and Harry P. Hatry, "Performance Monitoring and Reporting by Public Organizations", Discussion Paper for Proposed National Academy of Public Administration Resolution, September 30, 1991.

O   Wise, Lois Recascino and Robert Agranoff, "Organizational Characteristics and Productivity Measurement in Research Organizations", **Public Productivity and Management Review**, Vol. XV, No. 1, Fall 1991. pages 1-17.

O   "Work Teams Have Their Work Cut Out for Them", **HRFocus**, January, 1993.
     page 24.

www.ingramcontent.com/pod-product-compliance
Lightning Source LLC
Chambersburg PA
CBHW081611170526

45166CB00009B/2922